MAKE IT YOURSELF!
BOTS & CIRCUITS

Kelly Coss

Checkerboard Library

An Imprint of Abdo Publishing
abdopublishing.com

abdopublishing.com

Published by Abdo Publishing, a division of ABDO, PO Box 398166, Minneapolis, Minnesota 55439. Copyright © 2018 by Abdo Consulting Group, Inc. International copyrights reserved in all countries. No part of this book may be reproduced in any form without written permission from the publisher. Checkerboard Library™ is a trademark and logo of Abdo Publishing.

Printed in the United States of America, North Mankato, Minnesota
062017
092017

THIS BOOK CONTAINS RECYCLED MATERIALS

Design: Sarah DeYoung, Mighty Media, Inc.
Production: Mighty Media, Inc.
Editor: Liz Salzmann
Cover Photographs: Mighty Media, Inc.
Interior Photographs: Mighty Media, Inc.; Shutterstock

The following manufacturers/names appearing in this book are trademarks: Crayola®, CVS®, Energizer®, Market Pantry™, Sharpie®

Publisher's Cataloging-in-Publication Data
Names: Coss, Kelly, author.
Title: Make it yourself! bots & circuits / by Kelly Coss.
Other titles: Make it yourself! bots and circuits | Bots and circuits
Description: Minneapolis, MN : Abdo Publishing, 2018. | Series: Cool makerspace | Includes bibliographical references and index.
Identifiers: LCCN 2016962440 | ISBN 9781532110665 (lib. bdg.) | ISBN 9781680788518 (ebook)
Subjects: LCSH: Makerspaces--Juvenile literature. | Handicraft--Juvenile literature.
Classification: DDC 680--dc23
LC record available at http://lccn.loc.gov/2016962440

TO ADULT HELPERS

This is your chance to assist a new maker! As children learn to use makerspaces, they develop new skills, gain confidence, and make cool things. These activities are designed to help children create projects in makerspaces. Children may need more assistance for some activities than others. Be there to offer guidance when they need it. Encourage them to do as much as they can on their own. Be a cheerleader for their creativity.

Before getting started, remember to lay down ground rules for using tools and supplies and for cleaning up. There should always be adult supervision when using a hot or sharp tool.

SAFETY SYMBOLS

Some projects in this book require the use of hot or sharp tools. That means you'll need some adult help for these projects. Determine whether you'll need help on a project by looking for these safety symbols.

HOT!
This project requires the use of a hot tool.

SHARP!
This project requires the use of a sharp tool.

CONTENTS

What's a
MAKERSPACE?

Can you picture a place busy with budding **engineers** at work? Every tool or material you could want is at your fingertips. The atmosphere buzzes with creativity as you and your fellow makers construct amazing projects.

This is a makerspace! It is an area where people come together to create all kinds of cool stuff. Makers share sparks of creativity. They love to learn something new. They work together to build buzzing robots, craft cool light-up art projects, and design super **circuits**. Are you ready to become a maker?

SUPPLIES

Here are some of the materials and tools you'll need to do the projects in this book.

batteries,
AA & D

battery, 3V
(CR2032)

binder clips

brass brads

chenille stems

copper wire, insulated
& uninsulated

cork

craft foam

craft knife

craft sticks

DC motor
with wires

hot glue gun &
glue sticks

LEDs, 3V or
higher

light bulbs,
2.2V

BOTS & CIRCUITS TECHNIQUES

needle-nose pliers

paper container with lid

plastic pulley

propeller

pushpins

spring clothespin

wire cutter & wire stripper

wooden skewers

To strip a wire, put the wire stripper over the wire. Gently squeeze the handles while moving the wire stripper toward the end of the wire. Don't squeeze too hard, or you will cut the wire! And don't try to strip too much **insulation** at once. Do it in small sections.

It's important to know which wires are **positive** and which are **negative**. Positive wires are usually red. Negative wires are usually black. Keep red and black electrical tape handy. If your wires are not red and black, mark the positive and negative wires with the tape.

LIGHT-UP CONSTELLATION

Build your favorite constellation out of LED lights!

WHAT YOU NEED

scissors

ruler

sturdy cardboard

newspaper

paint

foam brush

sheet of paper

pencil

pushpin

3V battery (CR2032)

LEDs, 3V or higher, one for each star

uninsulated copper wire

red & black electrical tape

star stickers

binder clip

1. Cut a piece of cardboard that is 9 by 16 inches (23 by 40 cm). Cover your work surface with newspaper. Paint one side of the cardboard. Let it dry.

2. Draw the constellation on a sheet of paper. Make a dot for each star. This is your template.

3. Place the template on the painted side of the cardboard. Make sure at least 4 inches (10 cm) of cardboard shows on one side. This is where the switch for the lights will go.

4. Use a pushpin to make a hole at each star in the constellation.

5. Turn the cardboard over. Draw a line 2 inches (5 cm) in from the switch side. Draw another line 4 inches (10 cm) in from the switch side.

Continued on the next page.

BRIGHT-EYED CLOTHESPIN MONSTER

Turn a clothespin into a cute little monster with glowing eyes.

WHAT YOU NEED

newspaper · paint · paintbrush · spring clothespin

4 pieces of insulated copper wire, each about 6 inches (15 cm) long

ruler · wire stripper · 2 LEDs, 3V or higher

red & black electrical tape · 3V battery (CR2032) · scissors

craft foam · markers · hole punch · craft glue · chenille stem

1. Cover your work surface with newspaper. Paint the clothespin. Let it dry.

2. Strip 1 inch (2.5 cm) of **insulation** off one end of two wires. Wrap a stripped end around the long **lead** of each LED. These are the **positive** leads.

3. Cover the wrapped wires with red electrical tape.

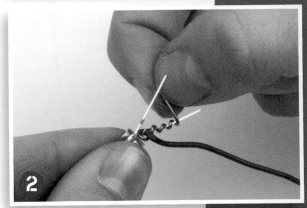

4. Strip 2½ inches (6 cm) off the other end of each wire. Twist the ends of the two wires together.

Continued on the next page.

 **TIP** Make sure the **voltage** of your LEDs is not lower than the battery's voltage. Otherwise the battery might burn out the LED.

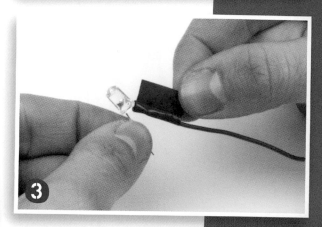

COLORING WIGGLE BIRD

This darling bird will draw cool colored lines as it dances and wiggles!

WHAT YOU NEED

4 washable markers

plastic cup

duct tape

D battery

3V DC motor with wires

electrical tape

scissors

penny

craft stick

cork

ruler

wire stripper

googly eyes, craft foam, feathers & other decorating items

sheet of paper

18

1. Duct tape the markers to the inside of the cup. Space them evenly. Line up the bottoms of the caps with the rim. Do not put tape over the caps.

2. Turn the cup over. Duct tape the battery to the bottom of the cup near the edge.

3. Set the motor next to the battery with the rod sticking up. Tape the motor to the battery with electrical tape.

4. Duct tape the penny to one end of the craft stick. Tape the other end of the craft stick to the side of the cork. Push the cork onto the motor's rod.

5. Strip 1 inch (2.5 cm) of **insulation** off each of the motor's wires. Use electrical tape to tape the **positive** wire to the battery's positive end.

6. Decorate the cup to look like a bird! Add feathers, wings, eyes, and a beak. Take the caps off the markers. Place the bird on a sheet of paper.

7. Tape the motor's **negative** wire to the battery's negative end. Watch your bird wiggle and draw!

FABULOUS FLASHLIGHT

This handy little light is powered by just a push!

1. Use a craft knife to cut an *X* in the top of the bottle cap. It should be just big enough so the light bulb fits securely into it.

2. Use a pushpin to make a small hole in the bottle cap near the edge.

3. Strip 1 inch (2.5 cm) of **insulation** off one end of the wire. Push the stripped end of the wire through the small hole from the top of the cap.

4. Strip 2½ inches (6 cm) off the other end of the wire. Wrap that end around the base of the bulb. Twist the wire to hold it in place.

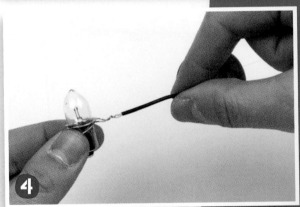

5. Push the base of the bulb into the *X* from the top of the cap.

6. Cover your work surface with newspaper. Use a needle-nose pliers to remove the end cap of the marker. Set the end cap aside.

7. Remove the inside and the tip of the marker.

Continued on the next page.

ROWDY DANCING ROBOT

Build a robot pal that moves and grooves while his nose spins 'round and 'round.

1. Cut two circles out of cardboard. Make them a little bigger than the bottle cap.

2 Hot glue the bottle cap to the center of a cardboard circle. Use a skewer to poke a hole through the center of the cap and cardboard.

3. Glue the other cardboard circle to the other side of the cap. Turn the cap over. Poke the skewer through the hole to make a hole in the second circle. Put the small rubber band around the bottle cap. It should be a little loose. This completes a pulley.

4 Cover the container with duct tape. Poke the skewer through the container a few inches below the top. Continue pushing it until it pokes through the other side. Wiggle the skewer around to make the holes bigger. Remove the skewer.

5 Cut a straw in half. Push each piece halfway through a hole in the container.

Continued on the next page.

PLAN A MAKER EVENT!

Being a maker is not just about the finished product. It is about communication, **collaboration**, and creativity. Do you have a project you'd like to make with the support of a group? Then make a plan and set it in action!

SECURE A SPACE

Think of places that would work well for a makerspace. This could be a library, school classroom, or space in a community center. Then, talk to adults in charge of the space. Describe your project. Tell them how you would use the space and keep it organized and clean.

INVITE MAKERS

Once you have a space, it is time to spread the word! Work with adults in charge of the space to determine how to do this. You could make an e-invitation, create flyers about your maker event, or have family and friends tell others.

MATERIALS & TOOLS

Materials and tools cost money. How will you supply these things? **Brainstorm** ways to raise money for your makerspace. You could plan a fund-raiser to buy needed items. You could also ask makers to bring their own supplies.

GLOSSARY

brainstorm – to come up with a solution by having all members of a group share ideas.

circuit – a path for an electric current created by a system of linked elements.

collaboration – the act of working with another person or group in order to do something or reach a goal.

engineer – someone who is trained to design and build structures such as machines, cars, or roads.

insulation – material used to keep something from losing or transferring electricity, heat, or sound.

lead – an electrical conductor, such as a wire, connected to an electrical device.

negative – related to a wire or end of a battery that energy flows toward when used in a circuit.

permission – when a person in charge says it's okay to do something.

positive – related to a wire or end of a battery that energy flows away from when used in a circuit.

voltage – electric force measured in volts.

WEBSITES

To learn more about Cool Makerspace, visit **abdobooklinks.com**. These links are routinely monitored and updated to provide the most current information available.

INDEX